AF322697

My special gift is
helping people and animals

Ben and
Finn's Playroom

↳ Benjamin, 7yo

My special gift is
making people laugh

KNOCK KNOCK
HA HA

↳ Finnegan, 5yo

My special gift is playing soccer
Christian, 6yo
My special gift is doing gymnastics and art
Isabella, 8yo

*This book is dedicated to my children ~ Ben and Finn*
*Their cousins ~ Isabella, Christian, Skylar, Andrew, Alexander, Darius, & Jasmine.*
*And my students*
*Believe in yourself, focus on your strengths, persevere,*
*And you will find your special gift*

**- Kara**

*To my parents, Akash and Kunal for supporting me in my journey to find my special gift*

**- Anchal**



This book may be ordered through booksellers or by contacting:

Kara Fleming
Karaleafleming@gmail.com


Hardcover ISBN - 9798218043957
Ebook ISBN - 9798218043971

# The Special Gift Fairy

Written By **Kara Fleming**

Illustrated by **Anchal Gupta**

You came to this earth one beautiful day.
Your loved ones were there to show you the way.

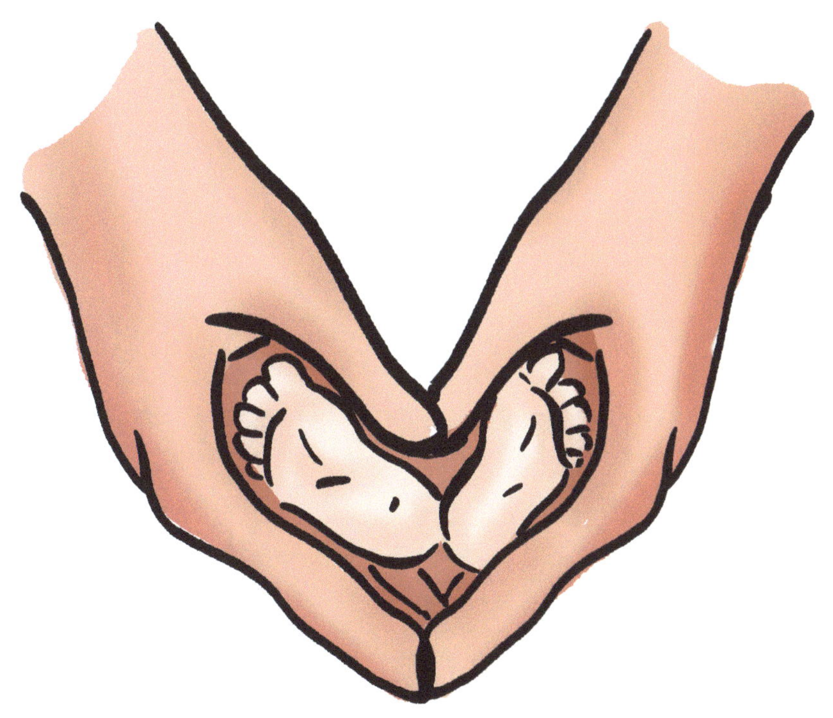

There was also a creature that no one could see,
but the Special Gift Fairy left suddenly.
The Fairy loves babies so very much,
she gave you a gift with her gentle touch.

Welcome
Baby Boy
Baboomian
9lbs 3oz
21 inches
March 4, 2016

What is your gift, your passion, or love
that blessed you at birth, and came from above?
What makes you happy and gives you some pep;
puts a smile on your face and bounce in your step?

Is it a skill, hobby, talent, or art,
that brings you joy, and fills up your heart?

Your gift lies inside you and is important to share.
Your loved ones will see it because they care.
Some gifts shine brightly and some hide inside,
Whatever your gift, just show it with pride.

Your gift makes you smile and helps others smile too.
It helps you feel better, when you're feeling blue.
Each gift you possess is special and unique;
Without your gift, life might seem bleak.

Don't be afraid to share what you love,
and remember that gift came from above.
So find out what makes you feel most alive.
Share it with others and continue to strive.

4B

Take pride in your strengths whatever they are,
share them with others, and you will go far.

Are you easy to talk to and make friends with ease?
Do you put others first to help try and please?

Are you funny? Do your jokes make others smile?
Are you creative, love fashion, or have great style?

In your home, do you like to take care of your pet?
Maybe someday you want to become a vet.

Do you love building blocks and Lego sets?
When you grow up you can manage construction projects.

If you love to watch birds, plant flowers, and be in nature,
Maybe someday you'll be a great landscaper.

In school, do you help your friends understand?
Teach them new ways so their knowledge expands?

A teacher by nature, shaping young minds.
To our precious future, of all different kinds.

Maybe you're gifted in reading and math,
Love babies and kids, but don't know the right path.
Caring and helpful, just make it your mission,
You might be a wonderful pediatrician.

What are the gifts
and talents you bring?

What makes you complete
and helps your heart sing?

At times we might feel like we can't compete,
With our friends or our siblings and feel incomplete.

Always remember you should not compare
Yourself to your friends because it's not fair.

Our talents are different. We are all unique.
All of our differences make life complete.
When you see other's shine, give them a cheer.
Be a good friend, loving sibling, and kind peer.

If you do not know what your gift may be,
It's okay, you're still young, there's much more to see.
You'll find out in time, be patient and wait.
Try new things, make new friends, don't hesitate.
Your gift is inside you, feel it and know
It fuels your spirit and helps you glow.

If you don't know your gift, please seek it out.
Ask family and friends who don't make you doubt,
The person you are and who you want to be.
You'll do great things someday, **believing** is key.

Write down some gifts that were given to you
From the Special Gift Fairy, just start with a few!

# Note to Parents and Educators

**The Special Gift Fairy** *encourages children to look within themselves to find their special gift.* The lessons and activities posted on the site below will help guide children in making good choices for themselves, in order to lead a happier and more fulfilling life. They will also serve as a reminder to us, as adults, that self-care and self-reflection are important, and are skills that we should model for our children.

Parent and Educator Activities & Resources at
**https://bodyandmindcounseling.com**

## Activity and Lesson Topics

★ Feelings
★ Perseverance
★ Positive Thoughts
★ Self Reflection
★ Taking Responsibility
★ Positive Attributes
★ Managing Strong Feelings
★ Coping Cards

Parent Resources

Teacher Resources

Dear Reader,

I'm asking that you please review my book on Amazon. I would greatly appreciate it!

Thank you,
Kara

My special gift is
making dinner for my family

Jasmine, 21yo

My special gift is
coloring

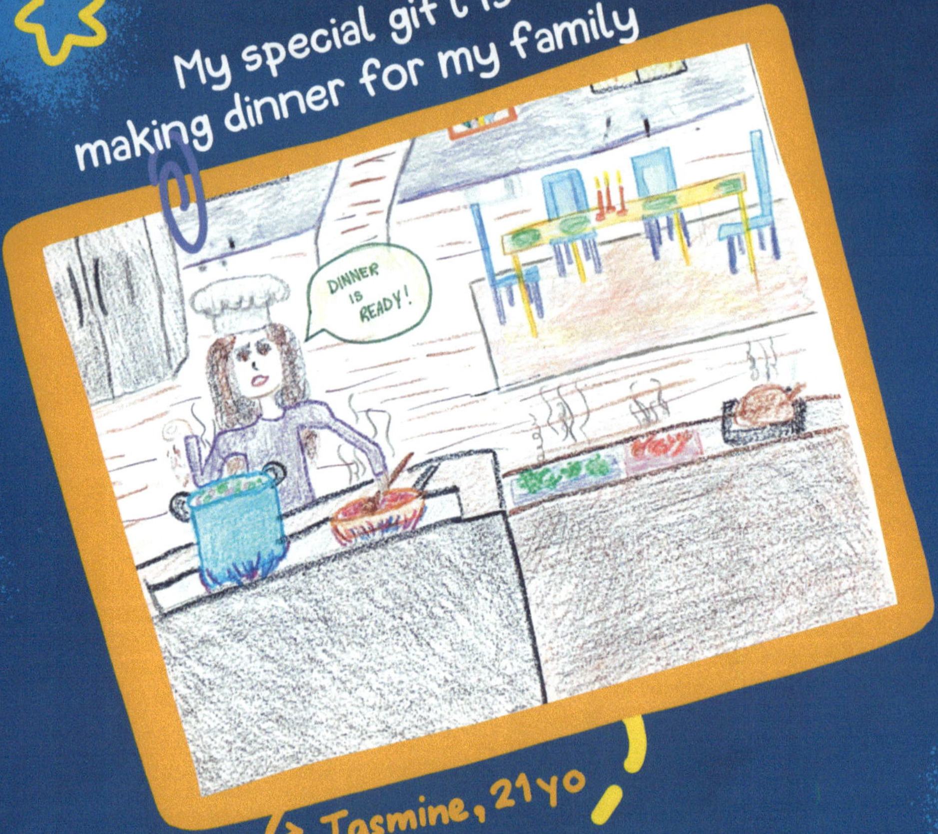

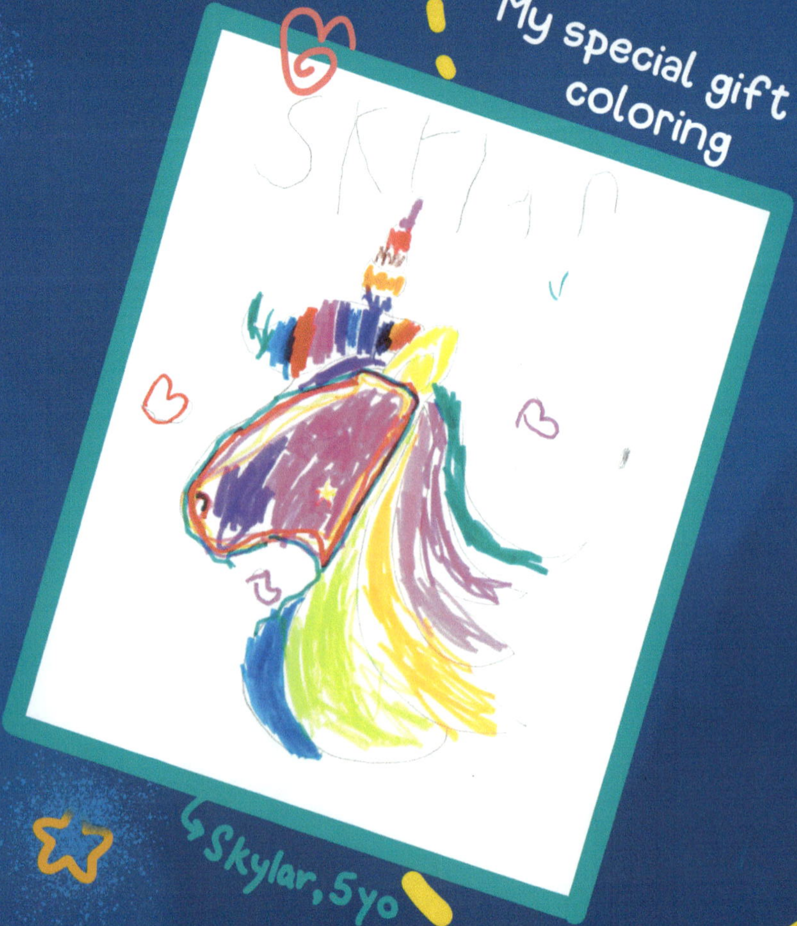

Skylar, 5yo

My special gift is helping people feel
better and be their BEST-SELF, both
mentally and physically